The Sleeping Prince

Written by Jenny Feely

Illustrated by Meredith Thomas

Flying Start
to Literacy®

Contents

Chapter 1:
Disaster strikes

The prince was in the garden when it happened. Suddenly he cried, "Ouch! Ouch! Ouch!"

The prince ran to the king.

"Something has bitten me!" he said. With that, he fell into a deep sleep.

"Wake up!" said the king. "Wake up!
What has bitten you?"

But the prince did not wake up.

Days passed, and still the prince slept. The king called all the wise men and all the wise women together.

"You must help the prince to wake up," he said. "He has been asleep too long and he is getting weaker and weaker."

But the wise men and women could not
wake the prince.

"Someone must know what to do,"
said the king.

So the king sent messengers out all over
the kingdom to find a cure.

Chapter 2:
A long journey

Mira lived at the very edge of the kingdom. She was very wise and she was also a special friend of all the animals. She could whisper to the animals and they could whisper to her. And that was how she had heard the message – a peregrine falcon had whispered in her ear.

When Mira heard about the sleeping prince, she said, "I know how to help him."

"I must go to the castle and wake the prince," she said.

Mira travelled across the land.
It was a long, hard journey.

When Mira reached the castle, she said,
"There are three things
that will wake the prince:
a pearl from the deep blue sea,
a golden fruit from the oldest tree
and a flower from the top of the tallest tree,
gathered at the greatest speed,
gathered for the greatest need."

But, the wise men and the wise women laughed.

10

"What nonsense!" said the king.

"Such nonsense!" said the wise men
and the wise women.

Chapter 3:
The greatest speed

Mira left the castle and went down to the beach.

"I must help the prince," Mira said. "I know where to find the three things, and I must get them here quickly."

Suddenly, Mira had an idea.

She called the sailfish that lived far out
at sea.

Mira whispered to the sailfish,
"You are the fastest animal in water.
Use your huge tail and strong body to speed
through the ocean and bring me a pearl
from the deep blue sea."

With a splash, the sailfish swam away.

Then, Mira whispered to the cheetah, "You are the fastest animal on the land. Bring me a golden fruit from the oldest tree."

The cheetah sprang off, its long body and strong muscles helping it to move swiftly.

14

Finally, Mira whispered to the
peregrine falcon,
"You are the fastest animal in the air.
Bring me a flower from the top of the
tallest tree.   And hurry!"

The peregrine falcon soared high into
the sky.

Chapter 4:

A pearl, a golden fruit and a flower

Soon, there was a large splash at the beach. The sailfish had returned, and in its mouth was a pearl from the deep blue sea. Mira returned to the castle.

Just as she reached the castle gate, the cheetah sprinted up to her. In its mouth it held a golden fruit from the oldest tree.

"Your great speed will save the prince," said Mira.

Then there was a loud screech from high in the sky. Mira looked up.

The peregrine falcon was speeding towards her. Its wings were tucked in, and it went faster and faster.

Then, at the last minute, it landed on Mira's arm. In its beak was a flower from the top of the tallest tree.

Chapter 5:
Just in time

Mira hurried into the castle.

"Here I have a pearl from the deep blue sea,
a golden fruit from the oldest tree
and a flower from the top of the tallest tree,"
said Mira. "All gathered at the greatest
speed, gathered for the greatest need."

"How can these things help the prince?"
asked the king.

"Yes," said the wise men and wise women.
"How can these things help?"

Mira placed the pearl in the prince's hands.
She placed the flower over the prince's heart.
Last of all, she placed a small piece of the
golden fruit on the prince's lips.

At first, nothing happened.

Then, the prince moved his lips and the fruit dropped into his mouth. He opened his eyes and sat up.

Everyone gathered around the prince. They clapped and cheered.

Everyone except for Mira. Her job was done.
Slowly, Mira walked out of the castle. The
cheetah and the peregrine falcon gathered
around and kept her safe all the way home.

A note from the author

I have always loved playing with traditional stories when I'm writing. I particularly like stories where impossible things happen.

So I asked myself, when might a peregrine falcon, a cheetah and a sailfish come together to save the day? This helped me to find a way to have the fastest animals in the world be part of a story. I hope you liked reading it as much as I liked writing it.